T0063299

HANDBOOK FOR UMRAH

HANDBOOK FOR UMRAH

Hashim Abd Ghani

PARTRIDGE

To order additional copies of this book, contact
Toll Free 800 101 2657 (Singapore)
Toll Free 1 800 81 7340 (Malaysia)
orders.singapore@partridgepublishing.com

www.partridgepublishing.com/singapore

Contents

بِسْمِ اللهِ الرَّحْمَنِ الرَّحِيمِ

In the Name of Allah, the Most Gracious, the Most Merciful

Preface

All praise and thanks are Allah's, Lord of Universe (mankind, jinn and all that exists). May the peace and blessing of Allah be upon Prophet Muhammad صَلَّى اللهُ عَلَيْهِ وَسَلَّم, His family and companions.

Umrah Handbook had been simplified for practical use and to be your companion while performing umrah pilgrimage in Mecca Al-Mukarrahmah and visiting Medina Al-Munawarah.

Rituals suggested in this handbook are not mandatory. It is desirable for pilgrims to do appropriate rituals within the teachings of Islam. The knowledge of performing umrah is of vital importance so that there will be no violations in implementing the pilgrimage. But if there are any, then pilgrims will be able to undertake the circumstances that will be required.

Handbook will provide step by step guidance starting with journey from home country until completion of pilgrimage. The guidance notes were arranged in nine parts.

Pilgrimage journey starts from the home country with undertaking the ethics of travelling. The vital part of umrah is to execute Five Pillars of Umrah, and it is sinful if it's not fulfilled. Umrah pilgrimage will be null and void, and compulsory to be repeated with penalties imposed.

The sequence of pilgrimage starts with State of Intend, Circumambulation (tawaf), Alternate Goings and Hair Clipping (saie and

2

tahallul). It is mandatory to perform Farewell Circumambulation (tawaf widak) before departing Mecca to other destination.

It is an obligation to visit Prophet Muhammad ﷺ at his tomb in Medina before or after performance of umrah.

It is advisable to read the Handbook prior to your departure for umrah pilgrimage, preferably with guidance of your religious teacher within your locality, seeking of what you do not understand.

Introduction

On my first umrah pilgrimage in 1990, the contents of my umrah handbook were mixed with long verses of Arabic recital rites and were in Malay. It is quite difficult to pronounce the Arabic verses for an average pilgrim, let alone to understand the meaning.

On arrival in Mecca, a religious leader (mutawif) was assigned to guide us throughout the pilgrimage. The religious leader instructed us to follow his rituals recitation for tawaf (circumambulation) and saie (alternate goings). Unfortunately for me, the ritual verses were different from my handbook. I faced difficulties in following long rituals recited by the religious leader. Furthermore with over-crowding of other pilgrims performing ritual, I lost my concentration and was separated from the main group.

As an umrah operator providing services for pilgrims, I found out that most pilgrims did not have required knowledge to perform umrah. The one-day guidance tutorial provided for pilgrims was insufficient, and they need a handbook for references.

Simplified and practical version in this handbook will provide minimum effort but maximum achievement in performing umrah pilgrimage. Handbook will be a useful reference, especially in reciting and understanding rituals.

Outcome of this handbook was achieved through guidance and consultation with my religious teacher, a commissioned hajj pilgrimage instructor. My experiences as an umrah operator and leader gave me added ability to prepare this handbook.

Umrah Submission Call
(Talbiah)

لَبَّيْكَ اللَّهُمَّ لَبَّيْكَ

لَبَّيْكَ لَا شَرِيْكَ لَكَ لَبَّيْكَ

إِنَّ الْحَمْدَ, وَالنِّعْمَةَ لَكَ وَالْمُلْكَ

لَا شِرِيْكَ لَكَ

O Allah, I have come to fulfil Your call; here I am.

I have come to fulfil Your call.
No confederacy upon You; here I am.

Verily, all praise and grace dominion are Yours.

No confederacy upon You.

Greetings (Selawat)
Invocation upon Prophet Muhammad ﷺ

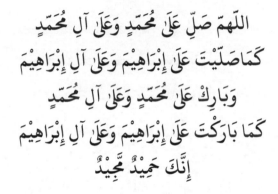

O Allah, may peace be upon
Prophet Muhammad and His family,

Just as how peace be upon
Prophet Ibrahim and His family,

O Allah, may blessings be upon
Prophet Muhammad and His family,

Just as how the blessings be upon
Prophet Ibrahim and His family,

Verily, Thou are the All-Praiseworthy and Most Honourable

Part 1

Pillars and Obligation of Umrah

Umrah is a pilgrimage to Baitullah al-Haram (Kaabah), Mecca performed by Muslims that can be performed at any time of the year, except during the months of hajj period, from 1 Syawal until before dawn of 10 Zulhijah Hijri Year. It is sometimes called 'minor pilgrimage', the hajj being 'major pilgrimage'.

In Islamic law (Syariat), umrah means to assume a sacred state (ihram) from a stated place (miqat) and perform.

a. Tawaf (circumambulation) is circling the Kaabah seven times in an anticlockwise direction.

b. Saie is between Al-Safa and Al-Marwah, seven alternate goings to and from, which is a symbolic re-enactment of Hajar's frantic search for water.

c. Tahallul (hair clipping and shaving) involves rituals that complete the umrah, and pilgrim will be free of sacred state (ihram) prohibitions.

In Arabic, the word 'umrah' is derived from I'timaar, which means a visit.

Performing umrah is highly recommended at least once in a lifetime for every able-bodied Muslim, as per the revelation by Allah the Almighty in the Noble Qur'an.

$$ \text{وَأَتِمُّوا الْحَجَّ وَالْعُمْرَةَ لِلَّهِ} .... (١٩٦) $$

7

"And perform properly (i.e., all ceremonies) according to the ways of Prophet Muhammad ﷺ the Hajj and Umrah [i.e., pilgrimage to Mecca] for Allah". (Al-Baqarah 2:196)

Hadith (describing words, actions, or habits) of Prophet Muhammad ﷺ by Bukhari, Muslim and others narrated that Prophet Muhammad ﷺ performed Umrah four times.

    a.   The umrah Hudaibiyah was during the month of Zulkaedah 6 Hijri Year, and it could not be performed by Prophet ﷺ and 1,500 companions due to being prevented from entering Mecca by Quarish polytheists.

    b.   The umrah Qada replaced umrah Hudaybiyah in the month of Zulkaedah 7 Hijri Year.

    c.   The umrah Ja'ranah was after the Battle of Hunain (Ghanimah) in the month of Syawal 8 Hijri Year.

    d.   The umrah during the hajj pilgrimage of Prophet Muhammad ﷺ was in the month of Zulkaedah 10 Hijri Year.

Pillars of umrah are mandatory practices that must be implemented in sequence. Umrah will be null and invalid if pillars are not fulfilled. Pilgrims who are not completing their practices of the pillars meant it's still on pilgrimage and is compulsory to be repeated. Penalty (dam) will be imposed, and imposition must be made in Mecca, and not in home country. Intended umrah cannot be cancelled arbitrarily, unless being prevented due to '*Phsar*' (i.e., being hinder by fears of enemy, epidemic diseases, natural disaster and etc.), but still bears penalty imposition so that the pilgrim can be out of sacred state.

Obligation of umrah is requirement that must be implemented accordingly. If not done, umrah is still valid but bears penalty (dam) as per stipulated conditions. Pilgrim will be required to execute two obligatory rites of the pillars of umrah. It is sinful to leave it intentionally.

Five Pillars of Umrah

Ser	Pillars of Umrah	Obligatory Rites
	Mandatory	Umrah is valid if any one of the rites is not implemented
a.	To state intent of umrah in your heart (niat)	To state intent of umrah at stated place (miqat)
b.	To do circumambulation (tawaf)	Duteous to thirteen prohibitions of sacred state (ihram)
c.	To do alternate goings (saie) between Al-Safa and Al-Marwah	–
d.	To do hair clipping/shaving (tahallul)	–
e.	To implement pillars in sequence	–
Notes:	Umrah will be null and void if not implemented	Pay a penalty as per stipulated conditions

Part 2

Ethics of Travel (Musafir)

It is desirable to undertake ethics of travel starting from your home before embarking to perform umrah. It is not mandatory, but it will put you in right mindset.

a. Take a purification bath with state of intent (niat), meaning, 'Solely, I undertake travelling bath because of Allah Taala.'

$$نَوَيْتُ الْغُسْلَ لِلسَّفَرِ لِلَّهِ تَعَالَى$$

b. Take ablutions, dressed up, and perform two sections prayers (salat) for travelling (musafir) with state of intent (niat), meaning, 'Solely, I perform travelling prayers two sections because of Allah Taala.'

$$أُصَلِّي سُنَّةَ السَّفَرِ رَكْعَتَيْنِ لِلَّهِ تَعَالَى$$

c. Recite rituals for travelling (musafir) after your prayers, meaning, 'In the Name of Allah, the Most Gracious, the Most Merciful. O Allah! Thou art a friend during the journey and security of my family, possessions, children, and friends. O Allah, protect me and others from any natural disaster and epidemic diseases.'

بِسْمِ اللهِ الرَّحْمَنِ الرَّحِيْمِ

اَللَّهُمَّ أَنْتَ الصَّاحِبُ فِي السَّفَرِ وَالْخَلِيْفَةُ فِي الْأَهْلِ وَالْمَالِ وَالْوَلَدِ

وَالْأَصْحَابِ، اَللَّهُمَّ احْفَظْنَا وَإِيَّاهُمْ مِنْ آفَاتِ الدُّنْيَا وَعَاهَاتِهَا

d. Recite rituals during your exit from the house: 'In the Name of Allah (I go), I put my trust in Allah. Not my efforts and strength except with permission of Allah.'

بِسْمِ اللهِ تَوَكَّلْتُ عَلَى اللهِ وَلَا حَوْلَ وَلَا قُوَّةَ إِلَّا بِاللهِ

e. Recite rituals before moving in the vehicle, meaning, 'Glory to Thee, O Allah, which has simplified it for our vehicle. Actually, we do not have the ability to control. We are all going back to our Lord.'

سُبْحَانَ الَّذِي سَخَّرَلَنَا هَـٰذَا وَمَا كُنَّا لَهُ مُقْرِنِيْنَ

وَإِنَّا إِلَى رَبِّنَا لَمُنْقَلِبُوْنَ

f. Recite rituals onboard the plane during take-off, meaning, 'In the name of Allah when departing and landing and at the time, surely our Lord is forgiving and merciful.'

بِسْمِ اللهِ مَجْرِيْهَا وَمُرْسَاهَا إِنَّ رَبِّي لَغَفُوْرٌ رَحِيْمٌ

Part 3

Stated Place (Miqat), State of Intent and Ihram Garbs

It must be stressed at very outset that there should be sincere intention to perform umrah, for all actions are judged by intentions. According to Hadith of the Prophet Muhammad ﷺ by Bukhari, the reward of deed depends on the intentions.

Stated place (miqat) is of two kinds.

    a. Timed (*zamani*):

        (1) Applicable during specific months for hajj pilgrimage from 1 Syawal until before dawn of 10 Zulhijah Hijri Year. Hajj pilgrimage will be invalid if not performed within this time limitation.

        (2) Applicable during any time of the year for umrah pilgrimage except during the months for hajj pilgrimage.

    b. Placement (*makani*): Designated locations for pilgrims intending to perform umrah or hajj. There are four locations of some distance from holy city of Mecca, where pilgrims must be in a state of ihram before crossing the boundaries.

        (1) Zulhulaifah (Bir Ali Mosque): The miqat is about 7 km from Medina and about 450 km from Mecca. This miqat is for pilgrims living in Medina and for those approaching Mecca from Syria, Egypt, Morocco, Spain, and other countries in that direction.

        (2) Qarnul Manazil: The miqat is a hilly place about 94 km to the east of Mecca. This miqat is for pilgrims from Nejd, Kuwait, and for those flying through the airspace

of that direction, including pilgrims coming from Malaysia, Indonesia, Brunei, and the surrounding areas.

(3)   Zatu Irqin: The miqat is about 94 km towards the northeast side of Mecca. This miqat is for pilgrims from Iran, Iraq, and for those coming from that direction.

(4)   Yalamlam: The miqat is a hilly area about 100 km to the southwest of Mecca. This miqat is for pilgrims from Yemen and others coming from that direction. It is also miqat for pilgrims from China, Japan, India, Pakistan, and Malaysia, who come by ship.

Muslims coming to Mecca with intention of performing umrah or hajj must not cross stated place (miqat) without state of intent and assuming into sacred state (ihram).

Pilgrims residing in stated place areas and Mecca will go to the following stated place (miqat) for hajj and umrah.

a. Tanaiem: A distance of 6 km from Mecca, on the way towards Medina.

b. Wadi Nakhlah: A distance of 41 km, from the east of Mecca in Iraq.

c. Ja'ranah: A distance of 24 km, to the east of Mecca.

d. Adah: A distance of 12 km, from Mecca to the south towards Yemen.

e. Hudaibiyah: A distance of 15 km from Mecca, towards the west. It is now known as Al-Shumaisi.

Wearing of ihram garb involves.

a. Wearing ihram garb in the home country if entering into Mecca first.

b. Wearing ihram garb in Medina if visiting (ziarah) Medina first. Then proceed to miqat Zulhulaifah (Bir Ali mosque) before performing umrah.

c. Take purification bath of ihram with state of intent (niat), meaning, 'Solely I undertake Ihram bath because of Allah Taala.'

$$نَوَيْتُ الْغُسْلَ سُنَّةَ اْلإِحْرَامِ لِلَّهِ تَعَالَى$$

d. For men, it is mandatory to only wear two pieces of unstitched cloth, preferably white.

e. Men to be dressed in iktibaak (covered left shoulder towards Kaabah) during circumambulation that is followed by Saie.

f. There is no restriction for women as long they are dressed up, covering forbidden parts of the body (aurat) as per Islamic law.

g. Men are to wear sandals or slippers without covering the toes and heels.

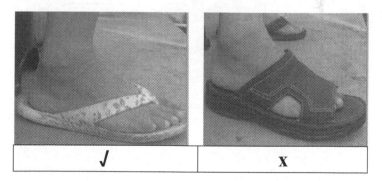

| ✓ | X |

Diagrammatic Locations of the Stated Place (Miqat)

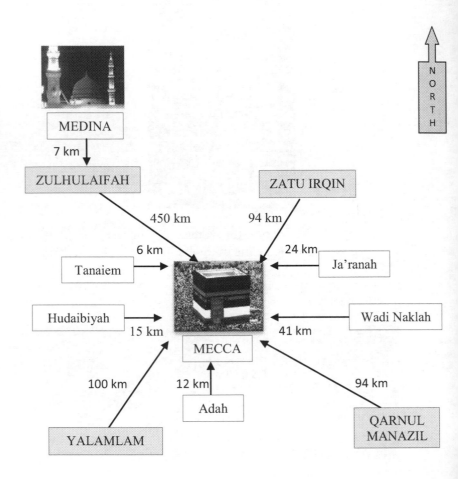

At miqat, make two sections prayers of *tahiyaltul* (sitting) at the mosque. Then make two sections prayers of sacred state (ihram) with intent (niat), meaning, 'Solely, I perform ihram prayers in two sections because of Allah Taala.'

$$أُصَلِّي سُنَّةَ الإِحْرَامِ رَكْعَتَيْنِ لِلَّهِ تَعَالَى$$

Declare intent of umrah and being in sacred state (ihram), meaning, 'Solely I am performing umrah and being in sacred state (ihram) because of Allah Taala.'

$$نَوَيْتُ العُمْرَةَ وَأَحْرَمْتُ بِهَا لِلَّهِ تَعَالَى$$

Pilgrim must declare intent of umrah and being in sacred state (ihram) before crossing the boundary of stated place (miqat).

Recite submission call (Talbiyah) at least three times; continue it with other recitals on the way to Mecca.

Once you are in sacred state (ihram), thirteen prohibitions will be duteous until completion of tahallul (hair clipping) rituals.

Thirteen Prohibitions of Scared State (Ihram)	
a.	To wear stitched clothes for men
b.	To cover face and head for men
c.	To wear gloves
d.	To use scent, perfume, and fragrance on your body and clothing
e.	To shave or clip hair from any part of the body
f.	To use hair cream
g.	To clip fingernails
h.	To indulge in sexual intercourse
i.	To indulge in preliminary action for sexual intercourse
j.	To get married (Ijab Qabul)
k.	To cut trees in Haram area (holy territories of Mecca and Medina)
l.	To hunt in Haram area (holy territories of Mecca and Medina)
m.	To wear footwear that covers toes and heels

Recommended optional undertakings in sacred state (ihram)

	Optional in Scared State (Ihram)
a.	To take purity bath before wearing ihram garb
b.	To do prayer (salat) of scared state (ihram)
c.	To put henna colouring on fingers (for women only)
d.	To state intend of umrah at stated place (miqat) prior to embarking on the journey to Mecca
e.	To recite submission call (Talbiyah) along the journey to Mecca
f.	To recite end portion of prayers (tasyahud) along the journey to Mecca, meaning, 'O Allah, grant blessings and peace upon Prophet Muhammad ﷺ and His family'.

Recite rituals before crossing the border-stone into Mecca, meaning, 'O Allah's sacred land, the land is your security. Protect me from fire, and give blessing at the day of Your call for servant.'

اَللّٰهُمَّ إِنَّ هَـٰذَا الْحَرَمَ حَرَمُكَ، وَالْبَلَدَ بَلَدُكَ وَالْأَمْنَ أَمْنُكَ، فَحَرِّمْنِي عَلَى النَّارِ، وَآمِنِّي مِنْ عَذَابِكَ يَوْمَ تُبْعَثُ عِبَادَكَ

Part 4

Circumambulation (Tawaf) of Kaabah

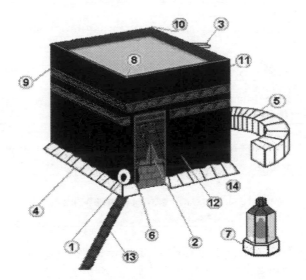

1. Hajar Aswad (Black Stone)
2. Kaabah Door
3. Meezab (rainwater spout made of gold)
4. Syarzawan (gutter)
5. Hijir Ismail
6. Multazam (space between Hajar Aswad and Kaabah Door)
7. Maqam Ibrahim عَلَيْهِٱلسَّلَام (Station of Ibrahim)
8. Hajar Aswad Corner (East)
9. Yamani Corner (South-West)
10. Syami Corner (North-West)
11. Iraqi Corner (North-East)
12. Kiswah (the cloth that covers the Kaabah)
13. Imaginary line adjacent to the green light on the wall marking the beginning and ending of circumambulation
14. Station of Jibril عَلَيْهِٱلسَّلَام

Circumambulation (Tawaf) is one of Islamic rituals during hajj and umrah pilgrimage. Muslims are to do circumambulation of Kaabah seven times in a counter-clockwise direction. Circumambulation of Kaabah is constantly on-going except during mandatory congregation prayers (salat). Kaabah symbolises focal direction of prayers for Muslims and not as a deity. The circling must begin (before) and end (after) at the point where the Black Stone (Hajar Aswad) is located. Prophet Muhammad ﷺ narrated that 70,000 angels are concluding request of blessings recital in between Yamani and Hajar Aswad corners. Kaabah front is a remarkable place for request of blessing from Allah سُبْحَانَهُوَتَعَالَى especially within Hijir Ismail. Kaabah should all times be to your left side. Do not turn your back, chest, or right arm towards Kaabah. If there is a turning of 360 degrees intentionally, then that particular round of circling will be null and should be replaced with another round. Pilgrims must be conversant with conditions of circumambulation.

It is desirable for pilgrims to undertake the following movement and rituals before embarking circumambulation.

   a.   Recite rituals before entering Grand Mosque (Masjidil Haram).

اَللَّهُمَّ أَنْتَ السَّلَامُ، وَمِنْكَ السَّلَامُ، فَحَيِّنَا رَبَّنَا بِالسَّلَامِ،

وَأَدْخِلْنَا الْجَنَّةَ دَارَ السَّلَامَ، تَبَارَكْتَ رَبَّنَا وَتَعَالَيْتَ يَا ذَا الْجَلَالِ

وَالْإِكْرَامِ، اَللَّهُمَّ افْتَحْ لِي أَبْوَابَ رَحْمَتِكَ وَمَغْفِرَتِكَ وَأَدْخِلْنِي فِيهَا،

بِسْمِ اللهِ وَالْحَمْدُ لِلَّهِ، وَالصَّلَاةُ وَالسَّلَامُ عَلَى رَسُوْلِ اللهِ،

صَلَّى اللهُ عَلَيْهِ وَسَلَّمَ

"O Allah, my Lord, You are only source of peace and prosperity, grant peace and prosperity into our hearts and admit us into haven of peace, glory, and exalted are You, Lord of Glory and Honour. O Lord, give me grace and forgiveness, enter us into it with the name of Allah. Praise for Allah. Peace and blessings be upon our Prophet Muhammad صَلَّى ٱللَّهُ عَلَيْهِ وَسَلَّمَ".

b.   Recite rituals on sighting Kaabah.

اَللهُ أَكْبَرُ، اَللهُ أَكْبَرُ، اَللهُ أَكْبَرُ،

لاَ إِلَهَ إِلاَّ اللهُ وَحْدَهُ لاَ شَرِيْكَ لَهُ،

لَهُ الْمُلْكُ وَلَهُ الْحَمْدُ وَهُوَ عَلَى كُلِّ شَيْءٍ قَدِيرٍ

"O Allah the Almighty, Allah the Almighty, Allah the Almighty. There is no God in truth except Allah, the One, no partner to Him. To Him belongs all dominion and praise, the only force behind all good. He has power over all things".

c.   Recite rituals while moving to Hajar Aswad (starting point for circumambulation).

بِسْمِ اللهِ، اَللهُ أَكْبَرُ، اَللَّهُمَّ إِيْمَانًا بِكَ، وَتَصْدِيْقًا بِكِتَابِكَ، وَوَفَاءً بِعَهْدِكَ، وَاتِّبَاعًا لِسُنَّةِ نَبِيِّكَ مُحَمَّدٍ صَلَّى اللهُ عَلَيْهِ وَسَلَّمَ

"In Your name, Allah is the Almighty. O Lord, I do circumambulation because of faith in Thee, for the truth of Your Book (Qur'an), and to fulfil promises according to Sunnah of Your Prophet Muhammad صَلَّى ٱللَّهُ عَلَيْهِ وَسَلَّمَ".

Mandatory for Circumambulation

a.	To do circumambulation with ablution
b.	Cleanliness of body, clothes, and circumambulation place of faeces
c.	Dressed up, covering 'aurat' (forbidden parts of your body, as per Islamic law)
d.	Circumambulation round begins (before) and ends (after) at the point of Hajar Aswad corner
e.	Make Kaabah on your left and move forward in an anti-clockwise direction
f.	Circumambulation with no other intentions
g.	Complete seven rounds with confidence
h.	Circumambulation outside Hijir Ismail and gutter of Kaabah (Syarzawan)

Optional for Circumambulation

a.	Men to be dressed in 'Iktibaak' (covered left shoulder toward Kaabah) for circumambulation followed by Saie
b.	Men can do light running for first three rounds of circumambulation (if permissible)
c.	Perform Istilam (raising right hand with opened palm facing Hajar Aswad and kiss the palm). Istilam towards Yamani corner without the kiss
d.	Recite rituals
e.	Complete seven rounds successively
f.	Circumambulation fervently and with esteem (tawadhuk)
g.	Make two sections of prayers after completion of circumambulation

Multi-Level Place for Circumambulation

Circumambulation of Kaabah:

a. State intent of circumambulation for *umrah* before crossing designated line alignment of *Hajar Aswad* and green light on the wall in the Grand Mosque *(Masjidil Haram)*.

اَللَّهُمَّ إِنِّي أُرِيْدَ طَوَافَ بَيْتِكَ الْحَرَامِ سَبْعَةَ
أَشْوَاطٍ طَوَافَ الْعُمْرَةِ لِلَّهِ تَعَالَى

"Solely, I perform circumambulation of umrah seven times around Kaabah because of Allah Taala".

b. Stating intent of circumambulation is not mandatory because it is inclusive in state of intent for umrah. It is desirable to state intent of circumambulation so as to remind that you are going for circling journey of Kaabah.

c. Complete seven rounds of circumambulation with confidence, following sequences and recital of rituals.

a. Make Istilam three times (raising right hand with opened palm facing Hajar Aswad and kiss your palm) before starting the circling, recite rituals.

(Three times) بِسْمِ اللهِ، اَللهُ أَكْبَرُ

"In the Name of Allah, Allah is the Almighty".

b. Recite rituals while circling from Hajar Aswad corner to Yamani corner.

أَسْتَغْفِرُ اللهَ الْعَظِيْمَ،

اَلَّذِي لَا إِلَـهَ إِلَّا هُوَ الْحَيُّ الْقَيُّوْمُ وَأَتُوْبُ إِلَيْه

"I beg forgiveness from Allah the Greatest. There is no deity but He, the Living, the Self-Subsisting, and I repent to Him".

c. Make Istilam three times (raising right hand with opened palm facing Yamani Corner without kissing) while moving and passing through Yamani Corner, recite rituals.

(Three times) بِسْمِ اللهِ، اَللهُ أَكْبَرُ

"In the Name of Allah, Allah is the Almighty".

d. Recite rituals from Yamani corner to Hajar Aswad corner.

رَبَّنَا أَتِنَا فِي الدُّنْيَا حَسَنَةً وَفِي الْأَخِرَةِ حَسَنَةً وَقِنَا عَذَابَ النَّارِ،
وَأَدْخِلْنَا الْجَنَّةَ مَعَ الْأَبْرَارِ،يَا عَزِيزُ يَا غَفَّارُ يَا رَبَّ الْعَالَمِينَ

"O Lord, grants us goodness in the world and hereafter, and protects us
from punishment of hellfire. O Lord the Victorious, the Forgiving, the
Lord of all Worlds, place us into heaven with the righteous".

**Second Circling - Tawaf
Circumambulation**

2

a. Make Istilam three times (raising right hand with opened palm
    facing Hajar Aswad and kiss your palm) while moving and
    passing through Hajar Aswad, recite rituals.

(Three times) بِسْمِ اللهِ، اَللهُ أَكْبَرُ

"In the Name of Allah, Allah is the Almighty".

b. Recite rituals while circling from Hajar Aswad corner to
    Yamani corner.

لَا إِلَهَ إِلَّا اللهُ وَحْدَهُ لَا شَرِيْكَ لَهُ،
لَهُ الْمُلْكُ وَلَهُ الْحَمْدُ يُحْيِي وَيُمِيْت بِيَدِهِ الْخَيْرُ،
إِنَّكَ عَلَى كُلِّ شَيْءٍ قَدِيْرٌ

"There is no deity but Allah the One, no partner for Him. The Eternal Owner of Sovereignty and all praise for Him, He gives life and causes death, He has all goodness. Verily, He is able to do all things".

c. Make Istilam three times (raising right hand with opened palm facing Yamani Corner without kissing) while moving and passing through Yamani Corner, recite rituals.

بِسْمِ اللهِ، اَللّهُ أَكْبَرُ (Three times)

"In the Name of Allah, Allah is the Almighty".

d. Recite rituals from Yamani corner to Hajar Aswad corner.

رَبَّنَا أَتِنَا فِي الدُّنْيَا حَسَنَةً وَفِي الْأَخِرَةِ حَسَنَةً وَقِنَا عَذَابَ النَّارِ،

وَأَدْخِلْنَا الْجَنَّةَ مَعَ الْأَبْرَارِ،يَا عَزِيزُ يَا غَفَّارُ يَا رَبَّ الْعَالَمِيْنَ

"O Lord, grants us goodness in the world and hereafter, and protects us from punishment of hellfire. O Lord the Victorious, the Forgiving, the Lord of all Worlds, place us into heaven with the righteous".

Second Circling - Tawaf Circumambulation **3**

a. Make Istilam three times (raising right hand with opened palm facing Hajar Aswad and kiss your palm) while moving and passing through Hajar Aswad, recite rituals.

بِسْمِ اللهِ، اَللّهُ أَكْبَرُ (Three times)

"In the Name of Allah, Allah is the Almighty".

b. Recite rituals while circling from Hajar Aswad corner to Yamani corner.

$$وَإِلَـٰهُكُمْ إِلَهٌ وَاحِدٌ لَا إِلَهَ إِلَّا هُوَ الرَّحْمَنُ الرَّحِيمُ$$

"And your Lord is the One. There is no deity but Him, the Most Gracious, the Most Merciful".

c. Make Istilam three times (raising right hand with opened palm facing Yamani Corner without kissing) while moving and passing through Yamani Corner, recite rituals.

$$(Recite three times) \quad بِسْمِ اللهِ، اَللهُ أَكْبَرُ$$

"In the Name of Allah, Allah is the Almighty".

d. Recite rituals from Yamani corner to Hajar Aswad corner.

$$رَبَّنَا أَتِنَا فِي الدُّنْيَا حَسَنَةً وَفِي الْأَخِرَةِ حَسَنَةً وَقِنَا عَذَابَ النَّارِ،$$
$$وَأَدْخِلْنَا الْجَنَّةَ مَعَ الْأَبْرَارِ، يَا عَزِيْزُ يَا غَفَّارُ يَا رَبَّ الْعَالَمِيْن$$

"O Lord, grants us goodness in the world and hereafter, and protects us from punishment of hellfire. O Lord the Victorious, the Forgiving, the Lord of all Worlds, place us into heaven with the righteous".

Fourth Circling - Tawaf Circumambulation

4

a. Make Istilam three times (raising right hand with opened palm facing Hajar Aswad and kiss your palm) while moving and passing through Hajar Aswad, recite rituals.

(Three times) بِسْمِ اللهِ، اَللهُ أَكْبَرُ

"In the Name of Allah, Allah is the Almighty".

b. Recite rituals while circling from Hajar Aswad corner to Yamani corner.

سُبْحَانَ رَبِّيَ الْعَظِيْمِ وَبِحَمْدِهِ

"Glory for Allah the Magnificent, the Praised One".

c. Make Istilam three times (raising right hand with opened palm facing Yamani Corner without kissing) while moving and passing through Yamani Corner, recite rituals.

(Three times) بِسْمِ اللهِ، اَللهُ أَكْبَرُ

"In the Name of Allah, Allah is the Almighty".

d. Recite rituals from Yamani corner to Hajar Aswad corner.

رَبَّنَا أَتِنَا فِي الدُّنْيَا حَسَنَةً وَفِي الْأَخِرَةِ حَسَنَةً وَقِنَا عَذَابَ النَّارِ،

30

وَأَدْخِلْنَا الْجَنَّةَ مَعَ الْأَبْرَارِ، يَا عَزِيْزُ يَا غَفَّارُ يَا رَبَّ الْعَالَمِيْنَ

"O Lord, grants us goodness in the world and hereafter, and protects us from punishment of hellfire. O Lord the Victorious, the Forgiving, the Lord of all Worlds, place us into heaven with the righteous".

Fifth Circling - Tawaf Circumambulation

a. Make Istilam three times (raising right hand with opened palm facing Hajar Aswad and kiss your palm) while moving and passing through Hajar Aswad, recite rituals.

بِسْمِ اللهِ، اَللهُ أَكْبَرُ (Three times)

"In the Name of Allah, Allah is the Almighty".

b. Recite rituals while circling from Hajar Aswad corner to Yamani corner.

لَا حَوْلَ وَلَا قُوَّةَ إِلَّا بِاللهِ الْعَلِيِّ الْعَظِيْمِ

"Not my efforts and strength except with permission of Allah the Most High, the Magnificent".

c. Make Istilam three times (raising right hand with opened palm facing Yamani Corner without kissing) while moving and passing through Yamani Corner, recite rituals.

بِسْمِ اللهِ، اَللهُ أَكْبَرُ (Three times)

"In the Name of Allah, Allah is the Almighty".

d. Recite the rituals from Yamani corner to Hajar Aswad corner.

رَبَّنَا أَتِنَا فِي الدُّنْيَا حَسَنَةً وَفِي الْأَخِرَةِ حَسَنَةً وَقِنَا عَذَابَ النَّارِ،
وَأَدْخِلْنَا الْجَنَّةَ مَعَ الْأَبْرَارِ،يَا عَزِيزُ يَا غَفَّارُ يَا رَبَّ الْعَالَمِينَ

"O Lord, grants us goodness in the world and hereafter, and protects us from punishment of hellfire. O Lord the Victorious, the Forgiving, the Lord of all Worlds, place us into heaven with the righteous".

Sixth Circling - Tawaf Circumambulation **6**

a. Make Istilam three times (raising right hand with opened palm facing Hajar Aswad and kiss your palm) while moving and passing through Hajar Aswad, recite rituals.

بِسْمِ اللهِ، اَللهُ أَكْبَرُ (Three times)

"In the Name of Allah, Allah is the Almighty".

b. Recite rituals while circling from Hajar Aswad corner to Yamani corner.

بِسْمِ اللهِ الرَّحْمَنِ الرَّحِيمِ

قُلْ هُوَ اللهُ أَحَدٌ ﴿١﴾ اللهُ الصَّمَدُ ﴿٢﴾

لَمْ يَلِدْ وَلَمْ يُولَدْ ﴿٣﴾ وَلَمْ يَكُنْ لَهُ كُفُوًا أَحَدٌ ﴿٤﴾

In the Name of Allah, the Most Gracious, the Most Merciful,
[1] "Say (O Muhammad ﷺ); He is Allah, (the) One.
[2] Allah the Self-Sufficient Master, Whom all creatures need, (He neither eats nor drinks).
[3] He begets not, nor He begotten.
[4] And there is none co-equal or comparable to Him".

c. Make Istilam three times (raising right hand with opened palm facing Yamani Corner without kissing) while moving and passing through Yamani Corner, recite rituals.

(Three times) بِسْمِ اللهِ، اَللهُ أَكْبَرُ

"In the Name of Allah, Allah is the Almighty".

d. Recite rituals from Yamani corner to Hajar Aswad corner.

رَبَّنَا أَتِنَا فِي الدُّنْيَا حَسَنَةً وَفِي الْأَخِرَةِ حَسَنَةً وَقِنَا عَذَابَ النَّارِ،
وَأَدْخِلْنَا الْجَنَّةَ مَعَ الْأَبْرَارِ، يَا عَزِيْزُ يَا غَفَّارُ يَا رَبَّ الْعَالَمِيْنَ

"O Lord, grants us goodness in the world and hereafter, and protects us from punishment of hellfire. O Lord the Victorious, the Forgiving, the Lord of all Worlds, place us into heaven with the righteous".

33

Seventh Circling - Tawaf Circumambulation

7

a. Make Istilam three times (raising right hand with opened palm facing Hajar Aswad and kiss your palm) while moving and passing and through Hajar Aswad, recite the rituals.

بِسْمِ اللهِ، اَللهُ أَكْبَرُ (Three times)

"In the Name of Allah, Allah is the Almighty".

b. Recite rituals while circling from Hajar Aswad corner to Yamani corner.

رَبَّنَا أتِنَا فِي الدُّنْيَا حَسَنَةً وَفِي الْأَخِرَةِ حَسَنَةً وَقِنَا عَذَابَ النَّارِ، وَأَدْخِلْنَا الْجَنَّةَ مَعَ الْأَبْرَارِ،يَا عَزِيزُ يَا غَفَّارُ يَا رَبَّ الْعَالَمِيْنَ

"O Lord, grants us goodness in the world and hereafter, and protects us from punishment of hellfire. O Lord the Victorious, the Forgiving, the Lord of all Worlds, place us into heaven with the righteous".

c. Make Istilam three times (raising right hand with opened palm facing Yamani Corner without kissing) while moving and passing through Yamani Corner, recite rituals.

بِسْمِ اللهِ، اَللهُ أَكْبَرُ (Three times)

"In the Name of Allah, Allah is the Almighty".

34

d. Recite rituals from Yamani corner to Hajar Aswad corner.

رَبَّنَا أَتِنَا فِي الدُّنْيَا حَسَنَةً وَفِي ٱلْأَخِرَةِ حَسَنَةً وَقِنَا عَذَابَ النَّارِ،
وَأَدْخِلْنَا الْجَنَّةَ مَعَ ٱلْأَبْرَارِ،يَا عَزِيزُ يَا غَفَّارُ يَا رَبَّ الْعَالَمِينَ

"O Lord, grants us goodness in the world and the hereafter, and protects us from punishment of hellfire. O Lord the Victorious, the Forgiving, the Lord of all Worlds, place us into heaven with the righteous".

Conclude circumambulation after passing Hajar Aswad corner with three Istilam (raising right hand with opened palm facing Hajar Aswad and kissing your palm) while moving, recite rituals.

(Three times) بِسْمِ اللهِ، اَللهُ أَكْبَرُ

"In the Name of Allah, Allah is the Almighty".

After completing circumambulation, recite rituals at Multazam (space in between Hajar Aswad Corner and Door of Kaabah), which is an efficacious place for reciting rituals. Multazam is normally crowded, it shall be sufficient to recite anywhere in Grand Mosque (Masjidil Haram) facing Multazam.

وَأُمَّهَاتِنَا وَإِخْوَانِنَا وَأَوْلَادِنَا مِنَ النَّارِ،
اَللَّهُمَّ أَحْسِنْ عَاقِبَتَنَا فِي ٱلْأُمُورِ كُلِّهَا وَأَجِرْنَا
مِنْ خِزْيِ الدُّنْيَا وَعَذَابِ ٱلْأَخِرَةِ،
اَللَّهُمَّ إِنِّي عَبْدُكَ وَابْنُ عَبْدِكَ وَاقِفٌ تَحْتَ بَابِكَ مُلْتَزِمٌ

بِأَعْتَابِكَ مُتَذَلِّلٌ بَيْنَ يَدَيْكَ،

أَرْجُو رَحْمَتَكَ وَأَخْشَى عَذَابَكَ، يَا قَدِيْمَ الْإِحْسَانِ،

اَللَّهُمَّ إِنِّي أَسْأَلُكَ أَنْ تَرْفَعَ ذِكْرِي وَتَضَعَ وِزْرِي

وَتُصْلِحُ أَمْرِي وَتُطَهِّرُ قَلْبِي وَتُنَوِّرَ لِي فِي قَبْرِي

الْجَنَّة وَتَغْفِرَ لِي ذَنْبِي، وَأَسْأَلُكَ الدَّرَجَاتِ الْعُلَى مِن

"O Allah, Lord of Al-Baitil Atiq (House), freedom to me, my father, my
mother, my relatives and children; distract us from punishment of hell. O
Allah, possessor of luxury, kindness, grace, and mercy, O Allah, beautify
the outcome in all our affairs and keep us from humiliation and torment
of Hereafter. O Allah, O Lord, this is real me, Thy servant and child,
standing before your door, humble before Thee with mercy and fear Ye
of Your trial. O Lord the All-Compassionate, I beg to mention my name
to be honoured. Drop my sins, cleanse my heart, and enlighten my grave
and forgive me. O Allah, I beg from You degrees of grades in heaven. O
Allah, Lord of Universe (mankind, jinn, and all that exists), please grant
my prayers".

Circumambulation Prayers:

a. Make two sections of prayers, if permissible within vicinity of
    the Station of Abraham (Maqam Ibrahim عَلَيْهِٱلسَّلَامُ) or any place
    within Grand Mosque (Masjidil Haram). Follow the practices
    (sunnah) by Prophet Muhammad صَلَّىٱللَّهُعَلَيْهِوَسَلَّمَ to recite Surah Al-
    Kafirun (the Disbelievers) in first section and Surah Al-Ikhlas
    (the Purity) in second section.

أُصَلِّي سُنَّةَ الطَّوَافِ رَكْعَتَيْنِ لِلَّهِ تَعَالَى

"Solely, I perform two sections of circumambulation prayers because of Allah Taala".

b.   Recite rituals after two sections prayers.

لَا إِلَهَ إِلَّا اللهُ الْحَلِيْمُ الْكَرِيْمُ، سُبْحَانَ اللهِ رَبِّ الْعَرْشِ الْعَظِيْمِ، اَلْحَمْدُ

لِلَّهِ رَبِّ الْعَالَمِيْنَ، أَسْأَلُكَ مُوْجِبَاتِ رَحْمَتِكَ، وَعَزَائِمَ

مَغْفِرَتِكَ،وَالْغَنِيْمَةَ مِنْ كُلِّ بِرٍّ، وَالسَّلَامَةَ مِنْ كُلِّ إِثْمٍ، وَالْفَوْزَ بِالْجَنَّةِ،

وَالنَّجَاةَ مِنَ النَّارِ، اَللَّهُمَّ لَا تَدَعْ لِي ذَنْبًا إِلَّا غَفَرْت إِلَّا فَرَجْتَهُ،

وَلَا دَيْنًا إِلَّا قَضَيْتَهُ، وَلَا مَرِيْضًا إِلَّا شَفَيْتَهُ،وَلَا ضَالًّ

ا إِلَّا هَدَيْتَهُ، وَلَا حَاجَةً مِنْ حَوَائِجِ الدُّنْيَا وَ الْأَخِرَةِ

إِلَّا قَضَيْتَهَا وَيَسَّرْتَهَا يَا رَبَّ الْعَالَمِيْنَ، يَا أَرْحَمَ الرَّاحِمِيْن

"There is no deity but Allah the Forbearing, the Generous. Glory on upon Allah, Lord of the Throne of Almighty. Praise upon Lord of Universe. I implore for Thou mercy and forgiveness, prompt blessing into our hearts to be survivor of sin, to be out of hell and rewarded with heaven. O Lord, do not leave us without forgiving even one sin unless it be forgiven by You, no debts unless cleared by You, no pain but what You heal, no leading astray but with guidance by You, none arising out of an intention on the world and hereafter unless Thou wish it fulfilled. The Lord of the Worlds, Lord is the best of blessings".

37

The pilgrims then proceed to the taps of Zam Zam water. Before drinking, facing towards the Kaabah and recite rituals.

بِسْمِ اللهِ الرَّحْمَنِ الرَّحِيْمِ

اللَّهُمَّ إِنِّي أَسْأَلُكَ عِلْمًا نَافِعًا، وَرِزْقًا وَاسِعًا، وَشِفَاءً مِنْ كُلِّ دَاءٍ

"In the Name of Allah, Most Gracious and Most Merciful, O Allah, I ask Thee for useful knowledge, of sustenance and healing for all diseases".

Location of *Zam Zam* Water

Proceed to Batan al-Wadi, designated place for next rituals of Alternate Goings and Hair Clipping (Saie and Tahallul).

Part 5

Alternate Goings and Hair Clipping
(Saie and Tahallul)

Safa Hill   Marwah Hill

Batan al-Wadi (Designated Place)

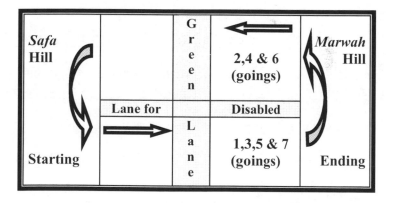

Saie ritual is seven times of alternately going between Safa and Marwah Hills, is an integral part of hajj and umrah, symbolizing the search for water by Hajar in order to give to her son, Prophet Ismail عَلَيْهِ ٱلسَّلَام. Prophet Ibrahim عَلَيْهِ ٱلسَّلَام was commanded by Allah سُبْحَانَهُوَتَعَالَى to leave his wife

Hajar and their infant son in the desert with only basic provisions to test their faith.

Conditions of Saie

a.	Do saie after completing circumambulation
b.	Start from Safa Hill and end at Marwah Hill
c.	Complete seven goings with confidence
d.	Reach designated ending of each going
e.	Do saie at Batan al Wadi (designated place)
f.	Do with intent for Saie only and no other

Optional Undertaking of Saie

a.	Enter through the door of al-Safa (Bab al Safa) to the place for Saie
b.	Face Kaabah for Takbir (call of Allah is Greatest) at Safa and Marwah Hill
c.	Do light running in between green light lane (for man)
d.	Do Saie goings in succession
e.	Be in state of ablutions
f.	Walk during the goings
g.	Recite rituals while walking

Movement and rituals of Saie are as follows:

a. State intent of Saie at Safa Hill before starting the goings.

اَللَّهُمَّ إِنِّي أُرِيْدُ أَنْ أَسْعَى بَيْنَ الصَّفَا وَالْمَرْوَةَ

سَبْعَةَ أَشْوَاطٍ سَعْيَ الْعُمْرَةِ لِلَّهِ تَعَالَى

"O Allah, I perform Saie of Umrah between Safa and Marwah seven times because of Allah Taala".

b. Recite rituals before starting the goings of Saie.

إِنَّ الصَّفَا وَالْمَرْوَةَ مِنْ شَعَائِرِ اللَّهِ، فَمَنْ حَجَّ الْبَيْتَ أَوِ اعْتَمَرَ

فَلَا جُنَاحَ عَلَيْهِ أَنْ يَطَّوَّفَ بِهِمَا، وَمَنْ تَطَوَّعَ خَيْرًا،

فَإِنَّ اللَّهَ شَاكِرٌ عَلِيمٌ. أَبْدَأُ بِمَا بَدَأَ اللهُ وَرَسُوْلُهُ،

"Verily, As-Safâ and Al-Marwah (two mountains in Mecca) are symbols of Allah. So it is not a sin on him who performs hajj or umrah (pilgrimage) in the House (Kaabah) to perform goings between them (As-Safa and Al Marwah). And whoever does voluntarily, verily, Allah is the All-Recognizer, All-Knower. I start (Saie) what Allah and His Messenger had begun".

Recite rituals while on the goings in following sequence.

41

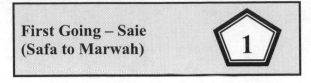

First Going – Saie (Safa to Marwah) **1**

a.   Recite rituals at Safa Hill before the going.

اَللهُ أَكْبَرُ، اَللهُ أَكْبَرُ، اَللهُ أَكْبَرُ،

لَا إِلَهَ إِلَّا اللهُ وَحْدَهُ لَا شَرِيكَ لَهُ،

لَهُ الْمُلْكُ وَلَهُ الْحَمْدُ يُحْيِي وَيُمِيتُ

وَهُوَ عَلَى كُلِّ شَيْءٍ قَدِيرٌ. لَا إِلَهَ إِلَّا اللهُ،

أَنْجَزَ وَعْدَهُ، وَنَصَرَ عَبْدَهُ، وَهَزَمَ الْأَحْزَابَ وَحْدَهُ

"Allah is the Almighty. Allah is the Almighty. Allah is the Almighty. There is no god worthy of worship but Allah, no partner to Him, and to Him all kingdoms and praise, He Who gives life and who causes death, and He who has power over all things. There is no god but the Lord, who fulfilled His promise and helped His slave, and He alone defeated the enemy". (Recite three times.)

b.   Recite rituals for first Saie while walking.

رَبَّنَا أَتِنَا فِي الدُّنْيَا حَسَنَةً وَفِي الْأَخِرَةِ حَسَنَةً وَقِنَا عَذَابَ النَّارِ

"O Lord, grants us goodness in the world and Hereafter, and save us from the torment of Fire".

c. Recite rituals in between green light lane (light running for men).

رَبِّ اغْفِرْ وَارْحَمْ، وَاعْفُ وَتَكَرَّمْ، وَتَجَاوَزْ عَمَّا تَعْلَمْ،

إِنَّكَ تَعْلَمُ مَا لَا نَعْلَمُ، إِنَّكَ أَنْتَ اللهُ الْأَعَزُّ الْأَكْرَمُ

"O Allah forgives us, have mercy on us, forgive us, grant us favours, and forgive us all that Thou know. Surely Thou know what we do not know and Thou are Lord of Majesty and Bounty".

d. Continue reciting rituals of first Saie until Marwah.

رَبَّنَا أَتِنَا فِي الدُّنْيَا حَسَنَةً وَفِي الْأَخِرَةِ حَسَنَةً وَقِنَا عَذَابَ النَّارِ

"O Lord, grants us goodness in the world and the Hereafter, and save us from the torment of Fire".

**Second Going – Saie
(Marwah to Safa)**   **2**

a. Recite rituals at Marwah Hill before the goings.

اَللهُ أَكْبَرُ، اَللهُ أَكْبَرُ، اَللهُ أَكْبَرُ،

لَا إِلَهَ إِلَّا اللهُ وَحْدَهُ لَا شَرِيْكَ لَهُ،

لَهُ الْمُلْكُ وَلَهَ الْحَمْدُ يُحْيِي وَيُمِيْتُ

وَهُوَ عَلَى كُلِّ شَيْءٍ قَدِيرٍ. لَا إِلَهَ إِلَّا اللهُ،

43

أَنْجَزَ وَعْدَهُ، وَنَصَرَ عَبْدَهُ، وَهَزَمَ الْأَحْزَابَ وَحْدَهُ

"Allah is the Almighty. Allah is the Almighty. Allah is the Almighty. There is no god worthy of worship but Allah, no partner to Him, and to Him all kingdoms and praise the kingdoms, He Who gives life and who causes death, and He who has power over all things. There is no but the Lord, who fulfilled His promise and helped His slave, and He alone defeated the enemy". (Recite three times.)

b. Recite rituals for second Saie while walking.

رَبَّنَا لاَ تُزِغْ قُلُوبَنَا بَعْدَ إِذْ هَدَيْتَنَا

وَهَبْ لَنَا مِنْ لَدُنْكَ رَحْمَةً إِنَّكَ أَنْتَ الْوَهَّابُ

"O Lord, let not our hearts deviate from the truth after Thou have guided us, and grant us mercy from Thou. Truly, Thou are Giver of All".

c. Recite rituals in between green light lane (light running for men).

رَبِّ اغْفِرْ وَارْحَمْ، وَاعْفُ وَتَكَرَّمْ، وَتَجَاوَزْ عَمَّا تَعْلَمُ،

إِنَّكَ تَعْلَمُ مَا لَا نَعْلَمُ، إِنَّكَ أَنْتَ اللهُ الْأَعَزُّ الْأَكْرَمُ

"O Allah forgives us, have mercy on us, forgive us, grant us favours, and forgive us all that Thou know. Surely Thou know what we do not know and Thou are Lord of Majesty and Bounty".

d.   Continue reciting rituals of second Saie until Safa.

$$رَبَّنَا لاَ تُزِغْ قُلُوبَنَا بَعْدَ إِذْ هَدَيْتَنَا$$

$$وَهَبْ لَنَا مِنْ لَدُنْكَ رَحْمَةً إِنَّكَ أَنْتَ الْوَهَّابُ$$

"O Lord, let not our hearts deviate from the truth after Thou have guided us, and grant us mercy from Thou. Truly, Thou are Giver of All".

**Third Going – Saie
(Safa to Marwah)**   **3**

a.   Recite rituals at Safa Hill before the goings.

$$اَللّٰهُ أَكْبَرُ، اَللّٰهُ أَكْبَرُ، اَللّٰهُ أَكْبَرُ،$$

$$لَا إِلَهَ إِلَّا اللّٰهُ وَحْدَهُ لَا شَرِيْكَ لَهُ،$$

$$لَهُ الْمُلْكُ وَلَهُ الْحَمْدُ يُحْيِيْ وَيُمِيْتُ$$

$$وَهُوَ عَلَىٰ كُلِّ شَيْءٍ قَدِيْرٍ. لَا إِلَهَ إِلَّا اللّٰهُ،$$

$$أَنْجَزَ وَعْدَهُ، وَنَصَرَ عَبْدَهُ، وَهَزَمَ الْأَحْزَابَ وَحْدَهُ$$

"Allah is the Almighty. Allah is the Almighty. Allah is the Almighty. There is no god worthy of worship but Allah, no partner to Him, and to Him all kingdoms and praise, He Who gives life and who causes death, and He who has power over all things. There is no but the Lord, who fulfilled His promise and helped His slave, and He alone defeated the enemy". (Recite three times.)

45

b. Recite rituals for third Saie while walking.

رَبَّنَا ظَلَمْنَا أَنْفُسَنَا وَإِنْ لَمْ تَغْفِرْ لَنَا
وَتَرْحَمْنَا لَنَكُونَنَّ مِنَ الْخَاسِرِينَ

"Our Lord, we have wronged our own souls, and if Thou forgives us and have mercy on us, surely we shall indeed be of those who perish".

c. Recite rituals in between green light lane (light running for men).

رَبِّ اغْفِرْ وَارْحَمْ، وَاعْفُ وَتَكَرَّمْ، وَتَجَاوَزْ عَمَّا تَعْلَمْ،
إِنَّكَ تَعْلَمُ مَا لَا نَعْلَمُ، إِنَّكَ أَنْتَ اللهُ الْأَعَزُّ الْأَكْرَمُ

"O Allah forgives us, have mercy on us, forgive us, grant us favours, and forgive us all that Thou know. Surely Thou know what we do not know and Thou are Lord of Majesty and Bounty".

d. Continue reciting rituals of third Saie until Marwah.

رَبَّنَا ظَلَمْنَا أَنْفُسَنَا وَإِنْ لَمْ تَغْفِرْ لَنَا
وَتَرْحَمْنَا لَنَكُونَنَّ مِنَ الْخَاسِرِينَ

"Our Lord, we have wronged our own souls, and if Thou forgive us and have mercy on us, surely we shall indeed be of those who perish".

46

Fourth Going – Saie (Marwah to Safa)

4

a. Recite rituals at Marwah Hill before the goings.

اَللهُ أَكْبَرُ، اَللهُ أَكْبَرُ، اَللهُ أَكْبَرُ،

لَا إِلَهَ إِلَّا اللهُ وَحْدَهُ لَا شَرِيْكَ لَهُ،

لَهُ الْمُلْكُ وَلَهُ الْحَمْدُ يُحْيِي وَيُمِيْتُ

وَهُوَ عَلَى كُلِّ شَيْءٍ قَدِيْرٍ. لَا إِلَهَ إِلَّا اللهُ،

أَنْجَزَ وَعْدَهُ، وَنَصَرَ عَبْدَهُ، وَهَزَمَ الْأَحْزَابَ وَحْدَهُ

"Allah is the Almighty. Allah is the Almighty. Allah is the Almighty. There is no god worthy of worship but Allah, no partner to Him, and to Him all kingdoms and praise, He Who gives life and who causes death, and He who has power over all things. There is no but the Lord, who fulfilled His promise and helped His slave, and He alone defeated the enemy". (Recite three times.)

b. Recite the rituals of the fourth Saie while walking.

اَللَّهُمَّ أَعِنِّي عَلَى ذِكْرِكَ وَشُكْرِكَ وَحُسْنِ عِبَادَتِكَ

"O Allah, help me to remember, cherish, and serve with good worship to Thee".

47

c. Recite rituals in between green light lane (light running for men).

رَبِّ اغْفِرْ وَارْحَمْ، وَاعْفُ وَتَكَرَّمْ، وَتَجَاوَزْ عَمَّا تَعْلَمْ،
إِنَّكَ تَعْلَمُ مَا لَا نَعْلَمْ، إِنَّكَ أَنْتَ اللهُ الْأَعَزُّ الْأَكْرَمُ

"O Allah forgives us, have mercy on us, forgive us, grant us favours, and forgive us all that Thou know. Surely Thou know what we do not know and Thou are Lord of Majesty and Bounty".

d. Continue reciting rituals of fourth Saie until Safa.

اَللَّهُمَّ أَعِنِّي عَلَى ذِكْرِكَ وَشُكْرِكَ وَحُسْنِ عِبَادَتِكَ

"O Allah, help me to remember, cherish, and serve with good worship to Thee".

Fifth Going – Saie (Safa to Marwah)	

a. Recite rituals at Safa Hill before the goings.

اَللهُ أَكْبَرُ، اَللهُ أَكْبَرُ، اَللهُ أَكْبَرُ،
لَا إِلَهَ إِلَّا اللهُ وَحْدَهُ لَا شَرِيْكَ لَهُ،
لَهُ الْمُلْكُ وَلَهُ الْحَمْدُ يُحْيِي وَيُمِيْتُ

وَهُوَ عَلَى كُلِّ شَيْءٍ قَدِيرٍ. لَا إِلَهَ إِلَّا اللهُ،
أَنْجَزَ وَعْدَهُ، وَنَصَرَ عَبْدَهُ، وَهَزَمَ الْأَحْزَابَ وَحْدَهُ

"Allah is the Almighty. Allah is the Almighty. Allah is the Almighty. There is no god worthy of worship but Allah, no partner to Him, and to Him all kingdoms and praise, He Who gives life and who causes death, and He who has power over all things. There is no but the Lord, who fulfilled His promise and helped His slave, and He alone defeated the enemy". (Recite three times.)

b.　Recite rituals of fifth Saie while walking.

أَسْتَغْفِرُ اللهَ، إِنَّ اللهَ غَفُوْرٌ رَّحِيْمٌ

"I beseech from Allah. Allah is the Forgiving, the Merciful".

c.　Recite rituals in between green light lane (light running for men).

رَبِّ اغْفِرْ وَارْحَمْ، وَاعْفُ وَتَكَرَّمْ، وَتَجَاوَزْ عَمَّا تَعْلَمْ،
إِنَّكَ تَعْلَمُ مَا لَا نَعْلَمُ، إِنَّكَ أَنْتَ اللهُ الْأَعَزُّ الْأَكْرَمُ

"O Allah forgives us, have mercy on us, forgive us, grant us favours, and forgive us all that Thou know. Surely Thou know what we do not know and Thou are Lord of Majesty and Bounty".

d.　Continue reciting rituals of fifth Saie until Marwah.

أَسْتَغْفِرُ اللهَ، إِنَّ اللهَ غَفُوْرٌ رَّحِيْمٌ

49

"I beseech from Allah. Allah is the Forgiving, the Merciful".

**Sixth Going – Saie
(Marwah to Safa)**

6

a. Recite rituals at Marwah Hill before the goings.

اَللّٰهُ أَكْبَرُ، اَللّٰهُ أَكْبَرُ، اَللّٰهُ أَكْبَرُ،

لَا إِلَهَ إِلَّا اللّٰهُ وَحْدَهُ لَا شَرِيْكَ لَهُ،

لَهُ الْمُلْكُ وَلَهُ الْحَمْدُ يُحْيِي وَيُمِيْتُ

وَهُوَ عَلَى كُلِّ شَيْءٍ قَدِيْرٍ. لَا إِلَهَ إِلَّا اللّٰهُ،

أَنْجَزَ وَعْدَهُ، وَنَصَرَ عَبْدَهُ، وَهَزَمَ الْأَحْزَابَ وَحْدَهُ

"Allah is the Almighty. Allah is the Almighty. Allah is the Almighty.
There is no god worthy of worship but Allah, no partner to Him, and to
Him all kingdoms and praise, He Who gives life and who causes death,
and He who has power over all things. There is no but the Lord, who
fulfilled His promise and helped His slave, and He alone defeated the
enemy". (Recite three times.)

b. Recite rituals for sixth Saie while walking.

سُبْحَانَ اللّٰهَ وَبِحَمْدِهِ، سُبْحَانَ اللّٰهِ الْعَظِيْمِ

"Glory and praised, exalted is He, Allah is Greatest".

50

c. Recite rituals in between green light lane (light running for men).

رَبِّ اغْفِرْ وَارْحَمْ، وَاعْفُ وَتَكَرَّمْ، وَتَجَاوَزْ عَمَّا تَعْلَمْ، إِنَّكَ تَعْلَمُ مَا لَا نَعْلَمُ، إِنَّكَ أَنْتَ اللهُ الْأَعَزُّ الْأَكْرَمُ

"O Allah forgives us, have mercy on us, forgive us, grant us favours, and forgive us all that Thou know. Surely Thou know what we do not know and Thou are the Lord of Majesty and Bounty".

d. Continue reciting rituals of sixth Saie until Safa.

سُبْحَانَ اللهِ وَبِحَمْدِهِ، سُبْحَانَ اللهِ الْعَظِيمِ

"Glory and praised, exalted is He, Allah is Greatest".

Seventh Going – Saie (Safa to Marwah)
7

a. Recite rituals at Safa hill before the goings.

اَللهُ أَكْبَرُ، اَللهُ أَكْبَرُ، اَللهُ أَكْبَرُ،

لَا إِلَهَ إِلَّا اللهُ وَحْدَهُ لَا شَرِيْكَ لَهُ،

لَهُ الْمُلْكُ وَلَهُ الْحَمْدُ يُحْيِي وَيُمِيْتُ

وَهُوَ عَلَى كُلِّ شَيْءٍ قَدِيْرٍ. لَا إِلَهَ إِلَّا اللهُ،

أَنْجَزَ وَعْدَهُ، وَنَصَرَ عَبْدَهُ، وَهَزَمَ الْأَحْزَابَ وَحْدَهُ

"Allah is the Almighty. Allah is the Almighty. Allah is the Almighty. There is no god worthy of worship but Allah, no partner to Him, and to Him all kingdoms and praise, He Who gives life and who causes death, and He who has power over all things. There is no but the Lord, who fulfilled His promise and helped His slave, and He alone defeated the enemy". (Recite three times.)

b. Recite rituals for seventh Saie while walking.

سُبْحَانَ اللّٰهِ، وَالْحَمْدُ لِلّٰهِ، وَلاَ إِلَهَ إِلاَّ اللّٰهُ، وَاللّٰهُ أَكْبَرُ،
وَلاَ حَوْلَ وَلاَ قُوَّةَ إِلاَّ بِاللّٰهِ الْعَلِيِّ الْعَظِيْمِ

"Glory to Allah, Praise to Allah, no deity but Allah, Allah is the Almighty. Not my efforts and strength except with permission of Allah the Most High and Greatest".

c. Recite rituals in between green light lane (light running for men).

رَبِّ اغْفِرْ وَارْحَمْ، وَاعْفُ وَتَكَرَّمْ، وَتَجَاوَزْ عَمَّا تَعْلَمْ،
إِنَّكَ تَعْلَمُ مَا لَا نَعْلَمُ، إِنَّكَ أَنْتَ اللّٰهُ الْأَعَزُّ الْأَكْرَمُ

"O Allah forgives us, have mercy on us, forgive us, grant us favours, and forgive us all that Thou know. Surely Thou know what we do not know and Thou are Lord of Majesty and Bounty".

d. Continue reciting rituals of seventh Saie until Marwah.

سُبْحَانَ اللهِ، وَالْحَمْدُ لِلّهِ، وَلاَ إِلَهَ إِلاَّ اللهُ، وَاللهُ أَكْبَرُ،

وَلاَ حَوْلَ وَلاَ قُوَّةَ إِلاَّ بِاللهِ الْعَلِيِّ الْعَظِيْمِ

"Glory to Allah, Praise for Allah, no deity but Allah, and Allah is the Almighty. Not my efforts and strength except with permission of Allah the Most High, the Magnificent".

Recite rituals after completion of Saie at Marwah Hill.

رَبَّنَا تَقَبَّلْ مِنَّا إِنَّكَ أَنْتَ السَّمِيعُ الْعَلِيمُ،

رَبَّنَا وَاجْعَلْنَا مُسْلِمِيْنِ لَكَ، وَمِنْ ذُرِّيَّتِنَا أُمَّةً مُسْلِمَةً لَكَ،

وَأَرِنَا مَنَاسِكَنَا، وَتُبْ عَلَيْنَا إِنَّكَ أَنْتَ التَّوَّابُ الرَّحِيمُ

"Our Lord, accept our deeds. Thou art the All-Hearing, All-Knowing. Our Lord, let us submissive unto Thee, let our offspring submissive unto Thee, to show us the ways and places of devotion, and to accept our repentance. Thou art the Oft-Returning, Most Merciful".

Tahallul (Hair Clipping and Shaving):

a. Recite rituals while holding the hair of your head.

اَللهُ أَكْبَرُ، اَللهُ أَكْبَرُ، اَللهُ أَكْبَرُ، اَللَّهُمَّ هَـٰذِهِ نَاصِيَتِي بِيَدِكَ،

فَاجْعَلْ لِي بِكُلِّ شَعْرَةٍ نُوْرًا يَوْمَ الْقِيَامَةِ،

وَاغْفِرْ لِي ذَنْبِي يَا وَاسِعَ الْمَغْفِرَةِ،

اَلْحَمْدُ لِلَّهِ الَّذِي قَضَىٰ عَنِّي نُسُكِي آتِنِي بِكُلِّ شَعْرَةٍ حَسَنَةً،

وَامْحُ عَنِّي بِهَا سَيِّئَةً، وَارْفَعْ لِي بِهَا دَرَجَةً،

وَاغْفِرْ لِي وَلِلْمُحَلِّقِينَ وَالْمُقَصِّرِينَ وَلِجَمِيعِ الْمُسْلِمِينَ،

اَللَّهُمَّ زِدْنِي إِيمَانًا وَيَقِينًا وَتَوْفِيقًا وَعَوْنًا،

وَاغْفِرْ لَنَا وَلِأَبَآئِنَا وَلِأُمَّهَاتِنَا وَلِأَزْوَاجِنَا وَلِأَوْلَادِنَا،

وَصَلَّى اللهُ عَلَىٰ سَيِّدِنَا مُحَمَّدٍ وَعَلَىٰ آلِهِ وَصَحْبِهِ وَسَلَّمَ

"Allah is the Almighty. Allah is the Almighty. Allah is the Almighty. O Lord, this is the top of my head in Your hand, so treat every hair as a light for me on the Day of Judgment and forgive my sins. O Lord, the Forgiver. All praises be to Allah who has perfected worship, prayers, to give charity with every strand of hair. Blot with a crime, take me to the ranks, and forgive me and those who shave, get haircuts, and all Muslims. O Allah, augment the faith and confidence, give me strength, help me, forgive me and my parents, wives, and children. Blessings and peace be upon our Master Muhammad ﷺ, His family and His companions".

b. Clip at least three strands of your hair, or shave it (for men). Women, clip hair at least the length of one roll over the finger.

c. Upon completing Tahallul rites, pilgrim will be free of sacred state (Ihram) prohibitions and umrah pilgrimage will be completed.

Flow Chart - Five Pillars of Umrah

FIVE PILLARS OF UMRAH				
1 → **STATE INTENT**	**2** → **TAWAF**	**3** → **SAIE**	**4** → **TAHALLUL**	**5** → **SEQUENCE**
↓	↓ PRACTICES &	MOVEMENT ↓	↓	↓
Purification Bath	Mandatory with Ablution	After completing Tawaf	Recite rituals while holding the Hair	
Wear Ihram Garb	Begins and Ends at Hajar Aswad Corner	At Designated Place (Batan al-Wadi)	Man to Clip at least Three Strands of Hair or Shave	Execute
Make Two Sections of Ihram Prayer	Kaabah on your Left, to Move Forward in Anti-Clockwise Direction	Starts from Safa Hill and Ends at Marwah Hill	Woman to Clip Hair with Length of One Roll over the Finger	Pillars in
State Intent in your Heart and being in Scared State	Moving outside of Hijir Ismail and Syarzawan (gutter of Kaabah)	Reach Designated Ending of each Going	Free of Scared State Prohibitions	Sequence
At or Before Crossing the Miqat	Complete 7 Rounds with Confidence	Complete 7 Goings with Confidence	Umrah Pilgrimage Completed	
Duteous to Thirteen Prohibitions				

Part 6

Historical Visit of Mecca Al-Mukarrahmah

Pilgrims will be able to visit historical sites in Mecca after completing Umrah.

a. **Jabal Al-Nur**: On one slope, there is a cave known as al-Ghar Hira (Cave of Hira), where Prophet Muhammad ﷺ received first revelation of Noble Quran from Angel Jibril عَلَيْهِٱلسَّلَامْ. The climb to the summit will take one hour before descending from opposite direction about twenty metres to the Cave of Hira.

Jabal (Mount*) Al-Nur*
(Location of *Hira* Cave)

b. **Jabal Thawr**: It is approximately four kilometres to the south of Grand Mosque. The mount holds the cave where Prophet Muhammad ﷺ and his companion Abu Bakar ibn Qhuhafah As-Siddiq رَضِيَٱللَّهُعَنْهُ took refuge for three nights in the

56

event of emigration to Medina. When Quraish came to look for them, Abu Bakar رَضِيَاللَّهُعَنْهُ worriedly told Prophet Muhammad صَلَّىاللَّهُعَلَيْهِوَسَلَّمَ that they were only two people, but Prophet صَلَّىاللَّهُعَلَيْهِوَسَلَّمَ assured him that Allah سُبْحَانَهُوَتَعَالَى was the third in the cave. When Quraish reached the cave, they thought that nobody could go into a cave with a spider-web spread across and birds nesting at entrance of the cave.

Jabal (Mount*) Thawr*

c. **Maulid Nabi**: Birthplace of Prophet Muhammad صَلَّىاللَّهُعَلَيْهِوَسَلَّمَ, known as Suq al-Layl or Shib Ali is towards the east of Grand Mosque. A new building was erected and is used as a library, known as Maktabah Mecca Al-Mukarramah.

d. **Maala Graveyard**: Located within one kilometre towards the east of the Grand Mosque. Here is the final resting place of the Mother of the Faithful Saidinatul Khadijah Kuwalid رَضِيَاللَّهُعَنْهَا, wife of Prophet Muhammad صَلَّىاللَّهُعَلَيْهِوَسَلَّمَ, His companions, and great ulama (Muslim religious leader). There were no indications to definite position of their graves.

Maala Graveyard

e. **Mount Arafah**: A granite hill in Arafah plain about twenty kilometres southeast of Mecca. Mount Arafah reaches about seventy metres in height and is also known as Mount of Mercy (Jabal ar-Rahmah). According to Islamic tradition, the hill is the place where Prophet Muhammad ﷺ stood and delivered Farewell Sermon to the Muslims during hajj towards the end of his life. On ninth of Dzulhijjah month, pilgrims from Mina will go to Arafah for the most important part of hajj. Here, Sermon of Hajj is narrated, Zuhur and Asar prayers are prayed together. Pilgrims spend whole day in Arafah, supplicating to Allah ﷾ to forgive their sins and praying for personal strength in future. It is an important place in Islam. Failure to be present in Plain of Arafah on required day invalidates the hajj pilgrimage. It was also narrated that Jabal ar-Rahmah was the meeting point where Prophet Adam ﵊ and Eve met after they descended from paradise. A monument was erected to signify it as a meeting point and a place of historic journey of Prophet Muhammad ﷺ, where he received final revelation of Allah as well as a complement for

58

the teachings of Islam. Many believed if they pray for a mate in Jabal Rahmah, the request will be granted.

Plain of Mount *Arafah*

Jabal ar-Rahmah

f. **Mina**: Known as "Tent City", situated five kilometres to the east of holy city of Mecca, stands on the road from Mecca to Plain of Arafah. Mina is best known for its role during annual hajj pilgrimage. More than 100,000 air-conditioned tents provide temporary accommodation to visiting pilgrims. In the valley of Mina is Jamarat Bridge, location of ritual for Stoning the Devil, performed between sunrise and sunset on last day of hajj, commemorating the occasion where Prophet Ibrahim عَلَيْهِٱلسَّلَامْ (Abraham) stoned the devil, that came between him and the command Allah سُبْحَانَهُوَتَعَالَىٰ had set him. Usually pilgrims will spend three nights in the Valley of Mina. This ritual occurs from eleventh to thirteenth of Zulhijjah month during hajj pilgrimage. At Mina, men and women are not allowed to sleep together.

Mina the "Tent City"

60

Part 7

Farewell Circumambulation
(Tawaf Widak)

Farewell circumambulation (Tawaf Widak) is to say goodbye to Kaabah with seven circling perfectly, but not followed by Saie. Follow the same procedures for circumambulation for umrah. The implementation is mandatory. Pilgrims need not to wear Ihram garbs as per umrah undertakings, but to be dressed up with proper attire covering forbidden parts of the body (aurat).

a. Recite intent of farewell circumambulation before starting the circling.

اَللَّهُمَّ إِنِّي أُرِيْدُ طَوَافَ بَيْتِكَ الْحَرَامِ سَبْعَةَ
أَشْوَاطٍ طَوَافَ الْوَدَاعِ لِلَّهِ تَعَالَى

"O Allah, solely I perform farewell circumambulation seven times, circling the Kaabah because of Allah Taala".

b. Make two sections of prayers upon completion of circumambulation. Follow same prayers (salat) procedures as per circumambulation.

c. Recite rituals after two sections of prayers.

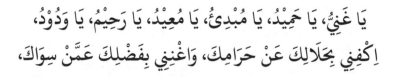

يَا غَنِيُّ، يَا حَمِيْدُ، يَا مُبْدِئُ، يَا مُعِيْدُ، يَا رَحِيْمُ، يَا وَدُوْدُ،
اِكْفِنِي بِحَلَالِكَ عَنْ حَرَامِكَ، وَاغْنِنِي بِفَضْلِكَ عَمَّنْ سِوَاكَ،

اَللَّهُمَّ اجْعَلْ خَيْرَ عُمُرِي آخِرَهُ، وَخَيْرَ عَمَلِي خَوَاتِمَهُ،
وَخَيْرَ أَيَّامِي يَوْمَ لِقَائِكَ

"O Rich One, O Praised One, O Originator, O Restorer, O All-Merciful, O Loving One, enrich me with what is permitted by You, keep me away from Your prohibitions, enrich me with grace, and prevent me from deviating from You. O Allah, make the best of my life until the end of life, the best act to end my time, and the best of the world that meet with Thou".

Recite rituals at Door of Kaabah (Multazam) before retreating.

اَللَّهُمَّ لَا تَجْعَلْ هَـٰذَا آخِرَ عَهْدِي بِبَيْتِكَ الْحَرَامِ،
وَإِنْ جَعَلْتَهُ آخِرَ عَهْدِي فَعَوِّضْنِي الْجَنَّةَ،
بِرَحْمَتِكَ يَا أَرْحَمَ الرَّاحِمِيْنَ

"O Allah, my Lord, let not this be last circumambulation and visit of mine at Baitullah. In the event it is destined to be last time, I request for heaven by Your favour, the Most Gracious, the Most Merciful".

Pilgrims are not to go shopping, photographing and other related activities after farewell circumambulation. All baggage will be readily packed at hotel lounge for loading onto transport for home journey. Pilgrims are allowed for natural calls and taking of meals while waiting for transfer to airport or other means to their home country. Restrictions will be lifted once pilgrims are out of Haram (forbidden) territories of Mecca.

Kaabah Door

Grand Mosque (*Masjidil Haram*)

Part 8

Penalty (Dam) for Umrah Only

In Arabic, *Dam* means blood, but for umrah it means certain livestock (camel, cow, buffalo, goat, sheep, and kibasy) that are slaughtered in replacement for penalties. Penalty (dam) is compulsory and will be imposed upon pilgrims if there are such violations.

    a.   Violating the Five Pillars of Umrah.

    b.   Not duteous to thirteen prohibitions in Scared State (Ihram).

    c.   Leaving Grand Mosque (Masjidil Haram) without farewell circumambulation (tawaf widak).

    d.   Prevented from completing umrah due to'*Phsar*'.

Four Categories of Penalty (Dam):

Ser	Category	Description
a.	**Tertib & Taqdir**	(1) Tertib means to pay penalty in sequence. Replacement and changes is permitted if unable to produce the determined items.
b.	**Tertib & Ta'dil**	(2) Ta'dil means unable to produce meals and to replace with fasting.
c.	**Takhyir & Ta'dil**	(3) Takhyir means payment of penalty can be selected from the determined items.
d.	**Takhyir & Taqdir**	(4) Taqdir means the conditions in items replacement.

Offences and Penalties:

Ser	Offences	Category	Penalty
a.	Not being in scared state at the stated place (miqat)	**Tertib & Taqdir**	(1) To sacrifice a sheep, kibasy or 1/7 of a camel, cow or buffalo
b.	Leaving Masjidil Haram without farewell circumambulation. Menstruated women are not penalized but should recite rituals outside Masjidil Haram		**if unable** (2) To fast for ten days (three days in Mecca and seven days in home country) **if unable** (3) Heir will bear the responsibility
c.	Being prevented from completing umrah due to 'Phsar' (i.e; being hindered by fears of enemy, epidemic diseases, natural disaster) Note: Hair clipping or shaving the head will be after livestock reach place of sacrifice	**Tertib & Ta'dil**	(1) To sacrifice a sheep, kibasy, cow or a camel as you can afford **if unable** (2) To provide replete meals to the poor that can be purchased with value of a sheep or kibasy

d.	Indulge in sexual intercourse before completion of umrah. Mandatory to perform umrah pilgrimage again	**Tertib & Ta'dil**	(1) To sacrifice a camel **if unable** (2) To replace with a cow or buffalo **if unable** (3) To replace with seven sheep or kibasy **if unable** (4) To provide replete meals to the poor that can be purchased with value of a camel **if unable** (5) To fast for number of days equable to the weight of basic grain that can be purchased with value of one camel

e.	Hunting in Haram (forbidden) territories of Mecca and Medina	**Takhyir & Ta'dil**	(1) To replace with comparably sized livestock and distribute the meat to the poor
f.	Cutting or uprooting tree in Haram (forbidden) territories of Mecca and Medina, except dead dried tree		**or** (2) To provide replete meals to the poor that can be purchased with value of comparably sized livestock
			or (3) To fast for number of days equable to the weight of basic grain that can be purchased with value of comparably sized livestock
g.	Wearing of stitched clothes for men	**Takhyir & Taqdir**	(1) To sacrifice a sheep, kibasy or 1/7 part of a camel, cow or buffalo
h.	Covering of faces and heads for men		

i.	Wearing gloves		**or**
j.	Using scent, perfume and fragrance on body and clothing		(2) To provide replete meal to 6 poor people
k.	Shaving or hair clipping from any part of the body		**or**
l.	Nails clipping		(3) To fast for three days

Distribution of livestock sacrifices, provision of replete meals and giving of alms to the poor in Mecca can be made through the local representatives, community leaders, or the mutawif elected by the pilgrims.

Part 9

Visit (Ziarah) Medina Al-Munawarrah

The Mosque of Prophet Muhammad ﷺ
(*Nabawi* Mosque)

It is desirable for pilgrims to visit Medina al-Munawwarah, 'the Enlightened City', before or after performing umrah. The city contains Masjid Nabawi (Prophet's Mosque), burial place of Islamic Prophet Muhammad ﷺ and is second holiest city of Islam after Mecca.

As narrated by Ibn Umar, the Messenger ﷺ of Allah said, 'The one who visits my grave has earned my intercession.'

Alongside tomb of Prophet Muhammad ﷺ are graves of Caliphs Abu Bakar ibn Qhuhafah As-Siddig رضي الله عنه (the verifier of truth) and Umar ibn al-Khattab Al-Farouk رضي الله عنه (the split between right and wrong).

Recite rituals before crossing the border-stone into Medina.

اَللّٰهُمَّ إِنَّ هٰذَا حَرَمُ نَبِيِّكَ وَقَدْ حَرَّمْتَهُ عَلَى لِسَانِهِ
صَلَّى اللهُ عَلَيْهِ وَسَلَّمَ، فَاجْعَلْهُ وِقَايَةً لِّي
مِنَ النَّارِ وَأَمَانًا مِنْ سُوْءِ الْحِسَابِ

"O Lord, this is sacred country of Your Messenger, deprived from the request of Prophet صَلَّى اللهُ عَلَيْهِ وَسَلَّمَ. May it guard me from hell, punishment, and removal of bad calculation of the last day".

Ethics of Visiting the Tomb of Prophet Muhammad صَلَّى اللهُ عَلَيْهِ وَسَلَّمَ :

a. Upon checking into your residence, take a bath first. Then dress beautifully and apply perfume before proceeding for visit to the Mosque of Prophet Muhammad صَلَّى اللهُ عَلَيْهِ وَسَلَّمَ.

b. Along the way to the mosque, recite greetings (selawat) invocation to Prophet Muhammad صَلَّى اللهُ عَلَيْهِ وَسَلَّمَ. Enter the mosque through the door of Babussalam with your right foot. Recite rituals before entering the mosque.

بِسْمِ اللهِ وَعَلَى مِلَّةِ رَسُوْلِ اللهِ،
رَبِّ أَدْخِلْنِي مُدْخَلَ صِدْقٍ وَأَخْرِجْنِي
مُدْخَلَ صِدْقٍ، وَاجْعَلْ لِّي مِنْ لَدُنْكَ سُلْطَانًا نَصِيْرًا،
اَللّٰهُمَّ صَلِّ عَلَى سَيِّدِنَا مُحَمَّدٍ وَعَلَى آلِ سَيِّدِنَا مُحَمَّدٍ،
وَاغْفِرْ لِي ذُنُوْبِي وَافْتَحْ لِي أَبْوَابَ رَحْمَتِكَ،

$$\text{وَأَدْخِلْنِي فِيهَا يَا أَرْحَمَ الرَّاحِمِيْنَ}$$

'In the name of Allah and religion of Allah, O Allah, give me an entrance of sincerity and an exit of sincerity, and give me victorious aid. O Allah, bless our Master Muhammad ﷺ and His family. Forgive my sins, and open the gates of mercy, O Lord the Most Merciful'.

    c.   Proceed to Raudhah, floored with green carpet. Entire mosque is floored with red carpet. Make two sections prayers of tahiyaltul (sitting) of the mosque, if permissible, in front of the pulpit of Prophet Muhammad ﷺ.

    d.   Upon completing prayers of tahiyaltul (sitting) of the mosque, proceed to the tomb of Prophet Muhammad ﷺ for your greetings invocation to Prophet Muhammad ﷺ and His companions.

Deliver greetings invocation to Prophet Muhammad ﷺ:

    a.   Vacate your heart of all things worldly, and be present in the heart of greatness and majestic of Prophet ﷺ and His love for yourself. This is because in practice pilgrims are spiritually facing His presence. Say greetings with a relatively calm voice.

    b.   Due to crowding and long queuing of pilgrims within tomb's area, it is sufficient to deliver greetings invocation facing the tomb while moving.

$$\text{اَلسَّلَامُ عَلَيْكَ أَيُّهَا النَّبِيُّ وَرَحْمَةُ اللهِ وَبَرَكَاتُهُ،}$$
$$\text{اَلصَّلَاةُ وَالسَّلَامُ عَلَيْكَ يَا رَسُوْلَ اللهِ،}$$

اللّٰهُمَّ اٰجِزْهُ عَنْ اُمَّتِهِ اَفْضَلِ الْجَزَاءِ

'May peace be upon You, O Prophet, with mercy and blessing of Allah, blessing and peace upon You, O Messenger of Allah, O Allah, bestow best of rewards for what He did to his people'.

c. Deliver greetings (salam) from other people to Prophet Muhammad ﷺ.

اَلسَّلَامُ عَلَيْكَ يَا رَسُوْلَ اللهِ وَرَحْمَةُ اللهِ وَبَرَكَاتُهُ مِنْ

"May peace be upon you, the great Prophet, the generous, the merciful, blessing of Allah be upon you, from ……….. (name of person)".

Tomb of Prophet Muhammad ﷺ

72

While still facing the tomb, move a few steps to the right and deliver greetings to Caliph Abu Bakar ibn Qhuhafah As-Siddiq رَضِىَٱللَّهُعَنْهُ.

اَلسَّلَامُ عَلَيْكَ يَا خَلِيْفَةَ رَسُوْلِ اللهِ،
وَالسَّلَامُ عَلَيْكَ وَرَحْمَةُ اللهِ وَبَرَكَاتُهُ

'Peace upon you, O first caliph of the Prophet, peace and blessings of Allah upon thee'.

Continue facing the tomb. Move a few steps to the right and deliver greetings to Caliph Umar ibn al-Khattab Al-Farouk رَضِىَٱللَّهُعَنْهُ.

اَلسَّلَامُ عَلَيْكَ يَا مُظْهِرَ ٱلْإِسْلَامِ، اَلسَّلَامُ عَلَيْكَ يَا فَارُوْقُ،
اَلسَّلَامُ عَلَيْكَ وَرَحْمَةُ اللهِ وَبَرَكَاتُهُ

"Peace upon you, who discloses an obvious manner of Islam. Peace upon you, who was given the title of Al-Farouk. Peace and blessings of Allah upon thee".

Head back to Raudhah al-Mutahharah and make prayers for repentance and for the good of you, parents, friends, and Muslims in general. As per sayings of Prophet Muhammad صَلَّىٱللَّهُعَلَيْهِوَسَلَّمَ, Raudhah is one of the gardens of heaven.

Devotions in Nabawi Mosque:

a. Be present at all times for mandatory prayers (salat) congregation.

b. If permissible, make prayers (salat) and rituals in Raudhah.

Raudhah

Historical Visit (Ziarah) in Medina:

a. **Mosque of Quba**: In outlying environs of Medina is the oldest mosque in the world, founded on piety (taqwa) by Prophet Muhammad ﷺ and accompanied by Abu Bakar ibn Qhuhafah As-Siddig رضي الله عنه upon their arrival in Medina on his emigration from Mecca. According to Islamic tradition, offering two sections of prayers in Quba Mosque is equal to a reward of performing one umrah. According to hadiths narrated by Ahmad ibn Hanbal, Al-Nasa'i, Ibn Majah and Hakim al-Nishaburi, Prophet Muhammad ﷺ said,

'Whoever makes ablutions at home and then goes and offers two sections prayers in Mosque of Quba, therein will be rewarded the reward of an umrah (the minor pilgrimage)'.

74

Mosque of *Quba*

b. **Qiblatain (Two Kiblat) Mosque**: Mosque of Two Kiblat is the place where Prophet Muhammad ﷺ received command to change direction (kiblat) of prayers (salat) from Jerusalem to Mecca, and entire prayers congregation changed direction in prayers (salat). Thus it uniquely contained two prayer niches (mihrab). The mosque was renovated, and old prayer niche facing Jerusalem was removed; the one facing Mecca remained. Qiblatain Mosque is among three earliest mosques in Islam's history, along with Quba Mosque and Al-Masjid al-Nabawi.

*Qiblatain (*Two *Kiblat)* Mosque

75

c. **Baqi Graveyard**: The graveyard, located to southwest of Nabawi Mosque, holds much significance and is also known as Jannatul Baqi, meaning 'Garden of Baqi'. Prophet Muhammad ﷺ prayed (doa) every time he passed it. Relatives and companions of Prophet Muhammad ﷺ were buried here. It is desirable to offer rituals.

اَلسَّلَامُ عَلَيْكُمْ دَارَ قَوْمٍ مُؤْمِنِيْنَ ، وَإِنَّا إِنْ شَاءَ اللهَ بِكُمْ لَاحِقُوْنَ. أَنْتُمْ سَلَفُنَا وَنَحْنُ بِالْأَثَرِ. يَغْفِرُ اللهُ لَنَا وَلَكُمْ وَيَرْحَمُ اللهُ الْمُسْتَقْدِمِيْنَ مِنْكُمْ وَالْمُسْتَأْخِرِيْنَ. اَللَّهُمَّ لَاتَحْرِمْنَا أَجْرَهُمْ وَلَا تَفْتِنَّا بَعْدَهُمْ وَاغْفِرْ لَنَا وَلَهُمْ ، اَللَّهُمَّ اغْفِرْ لِأَهْلِ الْبَقِيْعِ الْغَرْقَدِ

"May blessings be on you, O dwellers of the graves of who believe in Islam. We will follow you, you are people who have gone before us and we are following you, hopefully Allah forgive us and you and have mercy on them first, and the last, O Lord, do not deprive us of reward upon their practices and do not slander us after them . Forgive our sins and forgive their sins and dwellers of Al-Baqi".

Al-Baqi Graveyard at the background

d. **Graveyard of the Uhud Martyrs**: This is the grave of Uhud martyrs and that of Prophet Muhammad's ﷺ uncle, Saidina Hamzah رضي الله عنه, within Mount Uhud area. While you are there, please take a moment to recite rituals for the martyrs and reflect on their sacrifices that they have made for Islam.

اَلسَّلَامُ عَلَيْكَ يَا حَمْزَةُ عَمَّ رَسُوْلِ اللهِ .

اَلسَّلَامُ عَلَيْكَ يَا سَيِّدَ الشُّهَدَاءِ .

اَلسَّلَامُ عَلَيْكَ يَا أَسَدَ اللهِ وَأَسَدَ رَسُوْلِهِ،

اَلسَّلَامُ عَلَيْكَ يَا عَبْدَ اللهِ بْنَ جَحْشٍ.

اَلسَّلَامُ عَلَيْكَ يَا مُصْعَبَ بْنَ عُمَيْرٍ.

اَلسَّلَامُ عَلَيْكُمْ يَا شُهَدَاءَ أُحُدٍ.

اَلسَّلَامُ عَلَيْكُمْ بِمَاصَبَرْتُمْ فَنِعْمَ عُقْبَى الدَّارِ.

اَللَّهُمَّ أَجْزِهِمْ عَنِ الْإِسْلَامِ وَأَهْلِهِ أَفْضَلَ الْجَزَاءِ وَأَجْزِلْ شَوَابَهُمْ

وَأَكْرِمْ مَقَامَهُمْ وَارْفَعْ دَرَجَاتِهِمْ بِمَنِّكَ وَكَرَمِكَ

يَا أَكْرَمَ الْأَكْرَمِيْنَ.

"May peace be upon you, O Saidina Hamzah, uncle of the Prophet, may peace be upon you, O chieftain of martyrs, peace be upon you, O lion of Allah and of the Prophet. Peace be upon you, O Saidina Abdullah bin Jahsyi. Peace be upon you, O Saidina Mus'ab bin Umair. May peace be upon you, O person, who died in Battle of Uhud, blessing upon your patience for fighting against the enemy and upright of Islam, that is the best rewards you will receive from your Lord. O Allah, my Lord, multiplied reward for their adherence and sanctity of Islam. Upgrade their prestige with Thy mercy, O Lord, the most Gracious".

Graveyard of Uhud Martyrs

It is desirable to do farewell visit (Ziarah Widak) to Prophet Muhammad ﷺ before leaving Medina for your next destination. Follow same greetings procedures on arrival, and recite rituals outside of the mosque within vicinity of green dome area.

وَارْزُقْنِي إِلَيْهِ الْعَوْدَةَ فِي خَيْرٍ وَعَافِيَةٍ اللّٰهُمَّ لَا تَجْعَلْهُ آخِرَ الْعَهْدِ

مِنْ هَذَا الْمَكَانِ الشَّرِيْفِ وَسَلَامَةٍ إِنْ عِشْتُ إِنْ شَاءَ اللهُ جِئْتُ

وَإِنْ مُتُّ أَوْ دَعَتْ عِنْدَكَ شَهَادَتِي وَصِحَّةٍ وَأَمَانَتِي وَعَهْدِي وَمِيْثَاقِي

مِنْ يَوْمِنَا هَذَا إِلَى يَوْمِ الْقِيَامَةِ وَهِيَ أَنْ لَا إِلَهَ إِلَّا اللهُ وَحْدَهُ

لَا شَرِيْكَ لَهُ وَشَهَادَةُ أَنَّ مُحَمَّدًا عَبْدُهُ وَرَسُوْلُهُ

78

سُبْحَنَ رَبِّكَ رَبِّ ٱلْعِزَّةِ عَمَّا يَصِفُونَ
وَسَلَمٌ عَلَى ٱلْمُرْسَلِينَ وَٱلْحَمْدُ لِلَّهِ رَبِّ ٱلْعَٰلَمِينَ

"My Lord, do not let pilgrimage into this holy place be the last one. Grant to me opportunity to revisit this place in good health; if longevity is Allah's willing, I will come again. If it doomed, I have devoted to Thou with creed and as a covenant servant of this day until the end. I testify there is no deity to be worshiped but Allah, the One Lord who has no partners, and I bear witness that Prophet Muhammad ﷺ is Messenger of Allah. Peace to all Prophet عَلَيْهِمَاالسَّلَامٌ, and all praise be to Allah, the Lord of Universe (mankind, jinn and all that exists)".

Green Dome